Yellow Umbrella Books are published by Capstone Press
151 Good Counsel Drive, P.O. Box 669, Mankato, Minnesota 56002
www.capstonepress.com

Library of Congress Cataloging-in-Publication Data
Bauer, David (David S.)
    People change the land / by David Bauer.
    p. cm.
    Summary: Simple text and photographs explore ways in which people change the
land, from building houses and bridges to planting gardens.
    ISBN 0-7368-2929-6 (hardcover)—ISBN 0-7368-2888-5 (softcover)
    1. Civil engineering—Juvenile literature. 2. Land use—Juvenile literature.
[1. Land use.] I. Title.
TA149.B38 2004
624—dc21   2003010978

Editorial Credits
Editorial Director: Mary Lindeen
Editor: Jennifer VanVoorst
Photo Researcher: Wanda Winch
Developer: Raindrop Publishing

Photo Credits
Cover: Image Ideas; Title Page: Image Ideas; Page 2: Image Ideas; Page 3: PhotoDisc;
Page 4: Digital Vision; Page 5: Royalty-Free/Corbis; Page 6: Royalty-Free/Corbis; Page
7: PhotoDisc; Page 8: Corbis; Page 9: Macduff Everton/Corbis; Page 10: Digital Vision;
Page 11: Royalty-Free/Corbis; Page 12: Corbis Images; Page 13: Corel; Page 14:
Royalty-Free/Corbis; Page 15: Buddy Mays/Corbis; Page 16: Comstock

1 2 3 4 5 6 09 08 07 06 05 04

People Change the Land

by David Bauer

Consultant: Dwight Herold, EdD, Past President,
Iowa Council for the Social Studies

Yellow Umbrella Books

an imprint of Capstone Press
Mankato, Minnesota

People Change the Land

How are farms and cities alike? How are tunnels and bridges alike?

How are lakes and dams alike?
These are all ways that
people change the land.

Digging and Planting

Before people change the land, the land might look like this.

People change the land when they dig and plant. Farmers change the land to grow food.

Houses and Cities

People also change the land when they build. Building houses changes the land.

Building cities changes the land, too. What do you think the land was like before this city was built?

Bridges

Before people change the land, the land might look like this.

People change the land when they build bridges. Bridges let people visit both sides of the land.

Tunnels

A mountain is a tall piece of land. Before people change the land, a mountain might look like this.

People change the land when they build tunnels. People use tunnels to go through a mountain.

Dams

Before people change the land,
a river might look like this.

People change the land when they build dams. A dam controls the flow of a river.

Lakes

Sometimes people use dams to make lakes. Making lakes is another way that people change the land.

People make lakes to keep water in one place. Some of these lakes give us water to drink.

Change the Land!

Dig a hole! Plant a garden!
You can change the land!

Words to Know/Index

bridge—a structure built over a river, railway, or road so that people or vehicles can get to the other side; pages 2, 9

build—to make something by putting different parts together; pages 6, 7, 9, 11, 13

city—a very large or important town; pages 2, 7

dam—a strong barrier built across a stream or river to hold back water; pages 3, 13, 14

farm—an area of land with buildings on it used for growing crops or raising animals; page 2

garden—a place where flowers and vegetables are grown; page 16

plant—to put a plant or seed in the ground so that it can grow; pages 5, 16

tunnel—a passage built beneath the ground or water or through a mountain for use by cars, trains, or other vehicles; pages 2, 11

Word Count: 222
Early-Intervention Level: 15